D1361058

SHARK ZONE

MAKO SHARK

by Jody Sullivan Rake

Reading Consultant:
Barbara J. Fox
Reading Specialist
North Carolina State University

Content Consultant:
Deborah Nuzzolo
Education Manager
SeaWorld, San Diego

CAPSTONE PRESS
a capstone imprint

Blazers is published by Capstone Press,
151 Good Counsel Drive, P.O. Box 669, Mankato, Minnesota 56002.
www.capstonepub.com

 Books published by Capstone Press are manufactured with paper
containing at least 10 percent post-consumer waste.

Library of Congress Cataloging-in-Publication Data
Rake, Jody Sullivan.
  Mako shark / by Jody Sullivan Rake.
    p. cm.—(Blazers. Shark zone)
  Includes bibliographical references and index.
  Summary: "Describes the mako shark, including physical features, habitat, hunting, and role
in the ecosystem"—Provided by publisher.
  ISBN 978-1-4296-5016-8 (library binding)
  1. Mako sharks—Juvenile literature. I. Title. II. Series.

QL638.95.L3R353 2011
597.3'3—dc22
                                    2010002273

Editorial Credits
Lori Shores, editor; Juliette Peters, designer; Kelly Garvin, media researcher;
    Laura Manthe, production specialist

Photo Credits
Seapics/Andy Murch, 15; C&M Fallows, 18–19; Caterina Gennaro-Kurr, 6–7; Howard
    Hall, 5, 25; James D. Watt, 28–29; Jerry Allen, 12–13; Masa Ushioda, 20–21, 27;
    Richard Herrmann, cover, 9, 10–11
Shutterstock/artida; Eky Chan; Giuseppe_R, design elements
Tom Stack & Associates, Inc./Andy Murch, 16–17, 23

Essential content terms are **bold** and are defined on the page where they first appear.

TABLE OF CONTENTS

CHAPTER 1

FAST AND FURIOUS

A shiny blue flash streaks through the water. A shark with a crescent-shaped tail dashes after a mackerel.

crescent—a curved shape that looks like the moon when it is a sliver in the sky

The mackerel is fast, but not fast enough. It can't outswim the speedy **predator**. The mako shark swallows the mackerel whole.

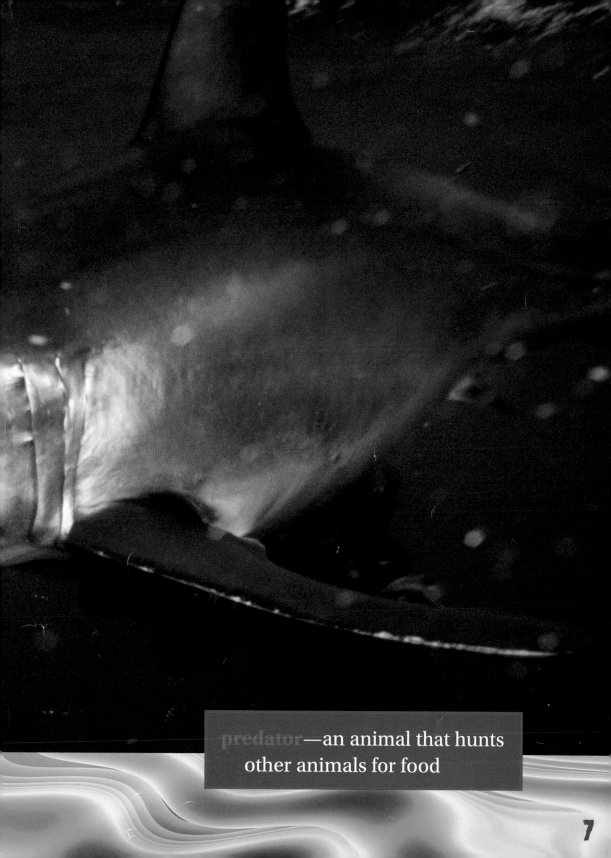

predator—an animal that hunts other animals for food

CHAPTER 2

BUILT FOR SPEED

Makos are the world's fastest sharks. They zip through the ocean at 22 miles (35 kilometers) per hour. They can reach speeds of 43 miles (69 kilometers) per hour when chasing prey.

prey—an animal hunted by another animal for food

SHARK FACT

Makos can leap 20 feet (6 meters) out of the water to catch prey.

Two types of mako sharks swim in the oceans. The shortfin mako and the longfin mako are both medium-sized sharks. They grow 8 to 10 feet (2.4 to 3 meters) long.

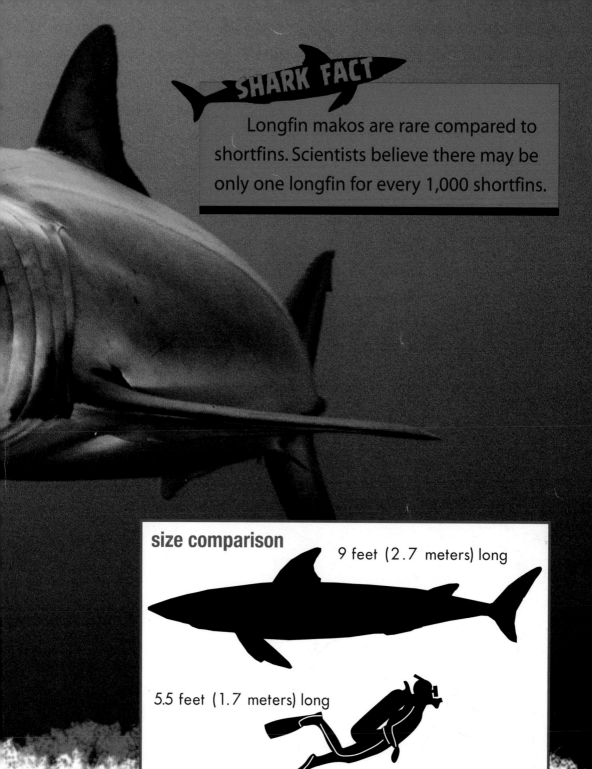

SHARK FACT

Longfin makos are rare compared to shortfins. Scientists believe there may be only one longfin for every 1,000 shortfins.

size comparison

9 feet (2.7 meters) long

5.5 feet (1.7 meters) long

dorsal fin

pectoral fin

The mako is built to be a high-speed hunter. It has a a pointed snout and a rocket-shaped body. A tall **dorsal fin** and narrow **pectoral fins** give the mako balance at high speeds.

snout

dorsal fin—the hard, flat body part that sticks up from the middle of a shark's back

pectoral fin—the hard, flat body part on either side of a shark

13

Mako sharks have strong tail fins for power and speed. Tail fin **keels** help makos move smoothly at fast speeds.

SHARK FACT

A mako's body temperature is warmer than the surrounding water. Its body temperature allows the shark to be more active.

keel—a ridge near the tail fin

tail fin

keel

Makos also use their power and speed to dive deep under water. They can swim as deep as 2,300 feet (701 meters).

Mako sharks have large eyes and great vision. These sharks can spot prey from far away. They can also see well with very little light.

SHARK FACT

Makos hunt by sight and use their speed to catch prey.

Makos feed on fast-swimming fish. They mainly hunt mackerels, tuna, and swordfish. Their long, sharp teeth grab and hold struggling prey.

SHARK FACT

Makos' teeth are not jagged like most meat-eating sharks. They are more useful for stabbing than slicing.

CHAPTER 3

THE MAKO'S WORLD

Makos stay mainly in deep, open waters. Shortfin makos live in warm waters worldwide. Longfin makos live in the western Atlantic Ocean. They also live in the middle of the Pacific Ocean.

Mako Sharks Range

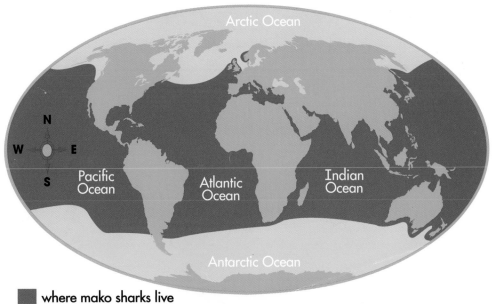

Arctic Ocean

N
W E
S

Pacific
Ocean

Atlantic
Ocean

Indian
Ocean

Antarctic Ocean

where mako sharks live

Like all sharks, mako sharks are important for a healthy ocean **ecosystem**. Makos don't compete with many other sharks for food. They hunt fish that are too fast for other sharks to catch.

ecosystem—a group of animals and plants that work together with their surroundings

CHAPTER 4

MAKOS AND HUMANS

Mako sharks rarely attack people. They usually swim in water that is too deep for swimmers or surfers. Most bites happen when people catch makos and pull them onto boats.

SHARK FACT

Out of the water, makos are the second most dangerous shark. Only great white sharks have attacked more people on boats.

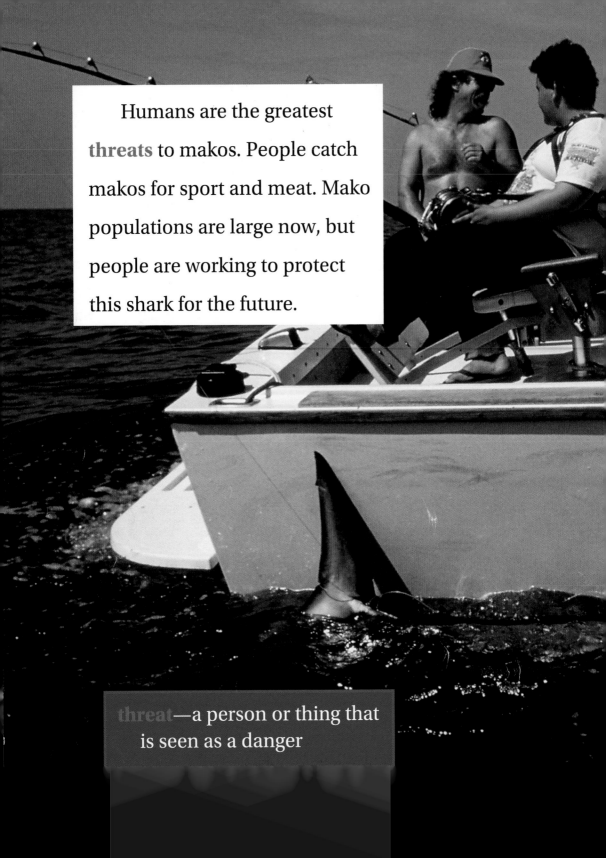

Humans are the greatest **threats** to makos. People catch makos for sport and meat. Mako populations are large now, but people are working to protect this shark for the future.

threat—a person or thing that is seen as a danger

SHARK FACT

Each year, people catch about 13 million pounds (6 million kilograms) of mako sharks.

Glossary

crescent (KRE-suhnt)—a curved shape that looks like the moon when it is a sliver in the sky

dorsal fin (DOR-suhl FIN)—the hard, flat body part that sticks up from the middle of a shark's back

ecosystem (EE-koh-sis-tuhm)—a group of animals and plants that work together with their surroundings

keel (KEEL)—a ridge along the surface of a fin

pectoral fin (PEK-tor-uhl FIN)—the hard, flat body part on either side of a shark

predator (PRED-uh-tur)—an animal that hunts other animals for food

prey (PRAY)—an animal hunted by another animal for food

threat (THRET)—a person or thing that is seen as a danger

Read More

Goldish, Meish. *Shark: The Shredder.* Afraid of the Water. New York: Bearport Publishing, 2010.

Randolph, Joanne. *The Mako Shark: Built For Speed.* Sharks: Hunters of the Deep. New York: PowerKids Press, 2007.

Smith, Miranda. *Sharks.* Kingfisher Knowledge. New York: Kingfisher, 2008.

Internet Sites

FactHound offers a safe, fun way to find Internet sites related to this book. All of the sites on FactHound have been researched by our staff.

Here's all you do:

Visit *www.facthound.com*

FactHound will fetch the best sites for you!

Index